Swahili in One Week

By Adam J. Weise

Edited by Sayi Michael

To my parents

HouseofBlueHope.org

House of Blue Hope raises funds, resources, social awareness, and provides other support for vulnerable children in Tanzania.

Helping children overcome poverty through education, House of Blue Hope provides housing, top-tier educational opportunities, and holistic support for children in its residential and educational facilities in Dar es Salaam, Tanzania.

AVCtanzania.org

Afri-Tanzania Volunteers for Change (AVC) is a youth-led volunteer organization designed to further community development in Tanzania by empowering youth through volunteer work. The organization works with volunteers from all over the world.

AVC was founded by a group of young men and women eager to uplift themselves from unemployment and poverty and to make positive changes within their communities. AVC empowers children and youth through education and volunteerism in order to mitigate poverty in Tanzania. AVC runs workshops, seminars, short-term and long-term volunteer programs, all of which are dedicated to helping youth find and reach their full potential.

Preface

How is this book different?

<u>Swahili in One Week</u> was designed to be accessible to anyone who does not yet speak a second language or doubt their ability to do so, but also useful for those interested in becoming advanced Swahili speakers.

Most introductory language guides include phrases and words but offer little understanding of the building blocks of the language. Such an approach is tiresome for the reader and suboptimal for those interested in continuing their language learning beyond rote memorization. <u>Swahili in One Week</u> instead sets you on the path to fluency by teaching you the fundamentals of Swahili, which you can use as a base for future learning. This book opts for the linguistic snowball effect - building upon each new word by identifying root words, underlying concepts, and the grammatical themes helps the reader take the first steps towards mastering the language.

Many language textbooks are full of unnecessary information and simply list words and phrases in an attempt to build fluency. Such a method guarantees the reader will:

    A. Waste your time learning the wrong words;

    B. Have difficulty retaining words because you do not use them in conversation;

    C. Struggle to conjugate verbs and build sentences;

    D. Fail to understand the cultural context in which to use vocabulary; and

    E. Become frustrated and want to quit

In <u>Swahili in One Week,</u> the reader will:

    A. Learn essential vocabulary with the option to dig deeper into subjects useful in daily life in Swahili-speaking countries like food and customs;

    B. Save time by using the included study plan;

    C. Obtain the ability to have brief exchanges after just one day; and

D. Communicate in the language in common situations after one week;

The reader—having no prior knowledge of Swahili—will gain the ability to manage basic exchanges and an understanding of the language upon that they can quickly build to become a proficient speaker. Thus, literal translations are used, by knowing "habari yako" means "news your" instead of "how are you," which is the non-literal translation, the language learner adds two unique words plus the phrase to their vocabulary.

Pronunciation Guide

The concept of a vowel having two sounds, which exists in English, does not in Swahili.

A – only "a" as in "car" in English or "anga" (sky) in Swahili

E – only "ay" as in "a,b,c" or "may" in English or "embe" (mango) in Swahili

I – only "ee" as in "bee" in English or "imba" (sing) in Swahili

O – only "oh" as in "go" in English or "ongea" (to talk) in Swahili

U – only "oo" as in "too" in English or "uma" (fork) in Swahili

There are a handful of letter combinations that make a sound that is unique and rarely heard in English. These take a lot of practice and are not crucial in early Swahili study.

Ng – "ng" as in "singing"

Practice Time

Reading without practice will result in understanding without fluency. It is key to spend each day practicing that day's contents and as well as the contents of prior days' lessons.

- Learn the day's lesson (2-10 minutes). If confused, reread the lesson no more than once, as the exercises will solidify your understanding.

- Complete the accompanying exercises (5-15 minutes) – this is the most crucial portion of the book.

- Lastly, use the preset vocabulary/phrase flashcards at the end of the lesson to choose six – ten new words/phrases to make your own (5-10 minutes). Finishing the exercises first is critical as the exercises will facilitate quick memorization of words. Use the flashcards English side first to memorize the six-ten words/phrases. Consider using memorization tactics such as:

- Visually imagining the word in Swahili and English.

- Thinking of a similar English word (ex. "mambo" in Swahili sounds similar to "mango" or the song "Mambo Number Five").

- Spelling the word.

- Saying the word out loud.

- Using the word in a sentence.

- An average language learner requires approximately ten exposures to a new word/phrase before acquiring it

Only with this level of dedication can one solidify past days' vocabulary and concepts while learning new lessons. Do the new exercises, repeat old exercises as needed, and, most importantly, get out of your comfort zone and speak with others. It is one thing to recall a word during a flashcard exercise, it is another to use it in a conversation. The majority of your time should be devoted to practice and speaking.

More About Swahili

Swahili, also called Kiswahili, is a Bantu language spoken in Tanzania, Kenya, Burundi, and Rwanda. Some of its words derive from English and Arabic, thereby giving speakers of those languages an advantage when learning Swahili. The vast majority of Swahili grammar rules are more logical and simpler than those of many other languages (like English); making it a great language for a beginning language learner.

Table of Contents

Day 1: Greetings/Replies

Greetings in Swahili are important and should be exchanged before even the simplest questions. Be prepared for repetitive greetings. Sometimes you will find yourself stating you are "fine" several times before moving on. Taking the time to properly greet someone demonstrates respect for that person and when done in Swahili, respect for their culture.

Greetings	Replies

Mambo vipi? – How are things/matters? .... Poa – Good, Safi – Clean

The following response is slang and should be reserved for use with "vijana" (young people) only.

Mambo vipi? – How are things? ....Shwari – (slang) Cool

"Mambo vipi" is often shortened to either the word "mambo" or "vipi" in common usage.

Mambo? – Things/Matters? .... Poa – Good, Safi – Clean, Shwari – Cool

Vipi? – How? .... Poa – Good, Safi – Clean, Shwari – Cool

"Habari" is often followed by a noun such as "nyumbani" (house).
Respond with "nzuri" or "salama."

Habari? – News? .... Nzuri – Good/Well

Gani – Which .... Salama - Peaceful

Leo – Today

Yako – Your

Habari yako? – News your?

Za - Of .... Salama – Peaceful

Habari za leo? – News of today? .... Njema – Good

Karibu – Welcome .... Asante – Thank you

Sana – Very

Karibu sana – Welcome very ....Asante sana – Thank you very much

The word "jambo" (thing) is a simplified greeting
commonly used with a "wazungu" (foreigners). Often
wazungu reply with "poa" but, let's instead learn the full
greetings and replies unbeknownst to most wazungu.

Jambo? [slang] – Matter/Thing/Problem? .... Sijambo – I do not have
things/problems (I am fine)

Hujambo? – You do not have things? .... Sijambo – I do not have
things/problems (I am fine)

Hamjambo? – You all do not have things?..Hatujambo – We do not have
things/problems (We are fine)

No actual feet touching/washing will take place despite the
translation of "shikamoo," which demonstrates respect
and is used when youths greet adults and when adults
greet elders. While it is a question, only children say
"shikamoo" with an intonation as adults pronounce it like
other declarative greetings such as "karibu."

Shikamoo – May I Touch/Wash Your Feet?........... Marahaba – I Accept You

Na + (any noun (ex. Nyumbani - house)? – And House? .... Nzuri – Good

Kwaheri – Goodbye...Kwaheri – Goodbye

Baadaye – Later ....Baadaye – Later

Safari njema – Trip Good ....Asante – Thank You

Pole – Sorry/Condolences ....Asante –Thanks

Samahani – Excuse Me .... Karibu – Welcome (all is well)

This greeting and reply is typically only used when entering
a building.

Hodi – Anyone There? ....Karibu – Welcome

This greeting and reply is typically only used in telephone
conversations.

Halo – Hello .... Mambo Vipi? – Matter/Thing How?

Greetings/Replies

Instructions: Cut out individual flashcards. The corresponding words align on the opposing page.

Habari	Safi
Mambo	Mambo vipi?
Nzuri	Sijambo
Jambo	Karibu
Poa	Salama
Asante	Marahaba
Asante sana	Hujambo
Hatujambo	Habari za leo?

Instructions: *Cut out individual flashcards. The corresponding words align on the opposing page.*

Clean	News
How is thing?	Thing
No thing	Good
Welcome	Thing
Peaceful	Good
I accept you	Thank you
You have a thing?	Thank you very much
News of the day?	We do not have a thing

Flashcards Chapter 1 – Part 2 – A

Greetings/Replies

Instructions: Cut out individual flashcards. The corresponding words align on the opposing page.

Habari yako?	Kwaheri
Mambo vipi?	Badi
Nzuri	Safari
Shikamoo?	Habari za leo?
Jambo?	Safari njema
Karibu	Na nyumbani kwako?
Poa	Sana
Marahaba	Karibu sana

Instructions: *Cut out individual flashcards. The corresponding words align on the opposing page.*

Goodbye	News your?
Later	Thing how?
Trip	Well
News of today?	May I touch Your feet?
Trip good	Thing?
And house your?	Welcome
Very	Good
Welcome very	I accept you

Greetings/Replies

Instructions: *Cut out individual flashcards. The corresponding words align on the opposing page.*

Salama	Samahani
Yako	Pole
Asante sana	Vipi?

Greetings/Replies

Instructions: Cut out individual flashcards. The corresponding words align on the opposing page.

Excuse me	Peaceful
Sorry	Your
How?	Thankful very

Common Phrases – Chapter 1 – Part 3 – A (Questions)

Greetings/Replies

Instructions: *Compose the following sentences in Swahili.*

How are you? .... ?

News? .... ?

May I touch your feet? .... ?

Good. ....

I accept you. ....

Welcome. ....

Thank you. ....

Sorry. ....

Common Phrases – Chapter 1 – Part 3 – B (Answers)

Greetings/Replies

Instructions: *Check your answers.*

How are you? .... Mambo vipi?

News? ....Habari?

May I touch your feet? ....Shikamoo?

Good.. .... Nzuri. Poa. Njema.

I accept you. ....Marahaba.

Welcome. ....Karibu.

Thank you. .... Asante.

Sorry. .... Pole.

Call & Reply – Chapter 1 – Part 4 – A (Questions)

Greetings/Replies

Instructions: Reply to the questions below with the appropriate Swahili phrase.

Q: Habari? .... A: ....

Q: Shikamoo? .... A: ....

Q: Mambo vipi? .... A: ....

Q: Karibu. .... A: ....

Q: Hujambo? .... A: ....

Q: Jambo? .... A: ....

Q: Mambo? .... A: ....

Q: Hodi? .... A: ....

Q: Pole? .... A: ....

Call & Reply – Chapter 1 – Part 4 – B (Answers)

Greetings/Replies

Instructions: Check your answers.

Q: Habari? .... A:.................................Nzuri/Salama.

Q: Shikamoo? .... A:....................................Marahaba.

Q: Mambo vipi?.................................... A:.................................Poa/Safi/Shwari.

Q: Karibu. .... A:.. Asante.

Q: Hujambo? .... A:.................................... Sijambo (1).

                                                     A:... Hatujambo (2+).

Q: Jambo? .... A:..................................... Sijambo (1)

                                                     A:... Hatujambo (2+).

Q: Mambo? .... A:.................................Poa/Safi/Shwari.

Q: Hodi? .... A:... Karibu.

Q: Pole? .... A:... Asante.

Day 2: Sentence Building Blocks

Possessives

Swahili possessives can be more complex than their English counterparts. Swahili has seven noun classes and possessives are modified in accordance with the noun class they modify. These noun classes are divided by word origin (ex. English noun class, Arabic noun class).

However, the class below is used by many Swahili speakers throughout their entire lives. Regardless of the noun class, you will be understood in full when using the following possessives:

Yangu	My
Yako	Your
Yake	His/Her
Yetu	Our
Yenu	You All's
Yao	Their

Formulating a Verb

Infinitive Verbs

Verbs yet to be conjugated always start with "ku"

Ex: Kusema (to say)

Verb Root

Drop "ku" from the infinitive

Ex: kusema's root is "sema"

Conjugation

Verb tenses will be covered in day 4, for now use "na" for present tense exclusively.

Three Questions Every Verb Answers in Its Three Parts (ex. "ninasema")

1. Who? – The beginning indicates the subject...ex. ni=I

2. When? – The middle indicates the tense...ex. na=now

3. What? – The root indicates the action...ex. sema=speak

Imperative/Command

Drop "ku" from the infinitive

Use the root word without conjugation

Ex. Sema – speak

Subject Prefixes and Pronouns

While pronouns are mandatory in English, pronouns (ex. she) are optional in the construction of sentences containing verbs in Swahili.

Pronoun/Subject English	Pronoun/Subject Swahili	Verb Subject	Verb Example
I	Mimi	Ni	Ninasema
You	Wewe	U	Unasema
He/She	Yeye	A	Anasema
We	Sisi	Tu	Tunasema
You all	Ninyi	M	Mnasema
They	Wao	Wa	Wanasema

Most Important Verbs to Know

Be prepared for the question "unatoka wapi?" (you from where?) to be asked frequently.

Kutoka ....To be from

Kwenda is an exception as the "kw" prefix is not dropped when it is conjugated.

Kwenda .... To go

Kula is an exception as the "ku" prefix is not dropped when it is conjugated.

Kula... To eat

Kusema .... To speak

Kutaka .... To want

Kufanya .... To do

Kulala ....To sleep

Kuona ....To see

Kulipa..To pay

Kuja.. To come/arrive/originate from

Kuwa .... To be

Kuweza .... To be able

Kupenda ....To like/love

Flashcards Chapter 2 – Part 1 – A

Sentence Building Blocks

Instructions: *Cut out individual flashcards. The corresponding words align on the opposing page.*

Mimi	Kufanya
Kutoka	Kusema
Wewe	Unasema
Kula	Yangu
Yeye	Kupenda
Yako	Yake
Sisi	Ninyi
Kuwa	Our

Sentence Building Blocks

Instructions: *Cut out individual flashcards. The corresponding words align on the opposing page.*

To do	I
To speak	To be from
You speak	You
My	To eat
To love/like	He/She
His/Her	Your
You all	We
Yetu	To be

Sentence Building Blocks

Instructions: *Cut out individual flashcards. The corresponding words align on the opposing page.*

Kulala	Wao
Ninatoka marekani	Ni
Kuja	Kwenda
Nilikuwa	Kutaka
Kuona	Tutakwenda
Kuweza	Sema
Unaweza?	Si
Kulipa	Yao

Sentence Building Blocks

Instructions: Cut out individual flashcards. The corresponding words align on the opposing page.

They	To sleep
Is/are	I am from America
To go	To come/originate from
To want	I was
We will go	To see
Speak (command)	To be able
Prefix for is/are not	Are you able?
Their	To pay

Common Phrases – Chapter 2 – Part 3 – A (Questions)

Sentence Building Blocks

Instructions: Fill in the blank – Questions.

You are from where? .... ?

You can do it? .... ?

Go! .... !

Speak. ....

He is good/ok. ....

News your? .... ?

You work which? .... ?

I am. ....

You go where? .... ?

You are American? .... ?

Common Phrases – Chapter 2 – Part 3 – B (Answers)

Sentence Building Blocks

Instructions: Fill in the blank – Answers.

You are from where? .... Unatoka wapi?

You can do it? .... Unaweza kufanya?

Go!.. .... Kwenda!

Speak.. .... Sema.

He is good/ok .... Yeye ni poa.

News your?.. .... Habari yako?

You work which? ....Unafanya kazi gani?

I am. ....Mimi ni.

You go where?.. .... Unaenda wapi?

You are American? ....Wewe ni marekani?

Day 3: Numbers

1 – 10

0	sifuri
1	moja
2	mbili
3	tatu
4	nne
5	tano
6	sita
7	saba
8	nane
9	tisa
10	kumi

11 – 20

11	kumi na moja
12	kumi na mbili
13	kumi na tatu
14	kumin na nne
15	kumi na tano
16	kumi na sita
17	kumi na saba
18	kumi na nane
19	kumi na tisa
20	ishirini

30 – 250

30	thelathini
40	arobaini
50	hamsini
60	sitini
70	sabini
80	themanini
90	tisini
100	mia moja
105	mia moja na tano
250	mia mbili hamsini

1,000 – 150,001

1,000	elfu moja
2,000	elfu mbili
10,000	elfu kumi
20,000	elfu ishirini
100,000	laki moja
200,000	laki mbili
1,000,000	milioni moja
2,000,000	milioni mbili
2,013	elfu mbili kumi na tatu
150,001	laki moja elfu hamsini na moja

Flashcards Chapter 3 – Part 1 – A

Numbers

Instructions: *Cut out individual flashcards. The corresponding words align on the opposing page.*

Mbili	Moja
Nne	Tatu
Sita	Tano
Nane	Saba
Kumi	Tisa
Kumi na Tano	Kumi na Moja
Ishirini na Tano	Ishirini
Hamsini	Thelathini

Numbers

Instructions: Cut out individual flashcards. The corresponding words align on the opposing page.

One	Two
Three	Four
Five	Six
Seven	Eight
Nine	Ten
Eleven	Fifteen
Twenty	Twenty Five
Thirty	Fifty

Numbers

Instructions: Cut out individual flashcards. The corresponding words align on the opposing page.

Mia Moja Hamsini na Tano	Mia Moja
Mia Mbili Hamsini	Mia Mbili
Elfu Moja Mia Nne	Elfu Moja
Elfu Kumi	Elfu Tatu
Elfu Hamsini	Elfu Kumi na Tano
Laki Tano	Laki Moja
Milioni Mbili	Milioni Moja
Milioni Kumi na Tisa	Milioni Tatu Mia Nane

Numbers

Instructions: *Cut out individual flashcards. The corresponding words align on the opposing page.*

100	155
200	250
1,000	1,400
3,000	10,000
15,000	50,000
100,000	500,000
1,000,000	2,000,000
3,000,800	19,000,000

Call & Reply – Chapter 3 – Part 3 – A

Numbers

Instructions: Reply to the questions below with the appropriate Swahili number.

Q: Una umri gani? / Una miaka mingapi?...A: ....

(How old are you?)

Q: Umezaliwa mwaka gani? ....A: .... :

(What year were you born?)

Q: Mpo wangapi kwenye familia yako? ......A: .... :

(How many siblings do you have?)

Q: Unasafiri kwa siku ngapi? ....A: .... :

(How many days are you traveling?)

Q: Namba ipi unaipenda?...........................A: .... :

(What is your favorite number?)

Q: Una watoto wangapi?............................A: .... :

(How many children do you have?)

Call & Reply – Chapter 3 – Part 3 – B (Responses)

Numbers

Instructions: *Reply to the questions below with the appropriate Swahili phrase.*

Q: How old are you?...........................A:...Thelathini (30).

Q: What year were you born? ....A:...Elfu mbili (2000).

Q: How many siblings do you have?...A: ....Mbili (2).

Q: How many days are you traveling? A:...Kumi (10).

Q: What is your favorite number?.......A:...Tisa (9).

Q: How many children do you have?...A: ....Moja (1).

Day 4: Shopping, Traveling and Past/Future

Tenses

Much in the Swahili-speaking world is negotiable with exceptions such as restaurants, hotels and large corporate stores. Some prices are inflated multiple times—negotiating is socially acceptable.

Bei gani?	Price which?
Noun, + Bei gani?	Noun, + Price which?
Hii, bei gani?	This, price which?
Hii, ndogo.	This, (too) small.
Hii, kubwa.	This, (too) big.
Ghali	Expensive
Tafadhali	Please
Kidogo	A bit
Bei yako ni ghali sana	Your price is high very
Punguza bei tafadhali	Reduce price please
Punguza bei kidogo	Reduce price a bit
Sitaki	I do not want
Asante lakini hapana	Thanks but no

Shillings are used as a measure of money in Uganda, Tanzania, and Kenya. Each country has its own currency and the shilling varies in value but the word "shilling" is used in each.

Shillingi	Shillings
/=	Shillings
Tsh/Ksh/Ush	Tanzanian/Kenyan/Ugandan Shillings

Repairs are done on a wide variety of products. Technicians for everything from damaged cell phones to flat tires are prevalent.

Fundi..Repairman/Technician

Teachers are highly respected in Swahili-speaking cultures. The first president of Tanzania was nicknamed "Mwalimu" and his picture is displayed in offices and shops.

Mwalimu .... Teacher

Daktari...Doctor

A very derogatory term in Swahili, shouting "mwizi" can literally cause a riot. Only use it in the case of a robbery.

Mwizi ....Thief

Food

Chakula ....Food

Chakula gani? .... Food which?

Chakula cha Asubuhi ....Food of Morning (breakfast)

Chakula cha Jioni .... Food of Evening (dinner)

Sahani ....Plate

Kisu ....Knife

Uma ....Fork

Kijiko ....Spoon

Chumvi ....Salt

Sukari...Sugar

Generally, tipping is not expected, but "bahashishi" is appreciated. Sometimes, wait staff will not return small change from a bill to the client with the hope that the client will allow them to keep it as a tip.

Bahashishi ....Gratuity

Moto...Hot

Baridi ....Cold

Maji ya moto ....Noun + ya + verb (hot/cold)

Nyama .... Meat

Kuku... Chicken

Mbuzi.. Goat

"Samaki" is sometimes fried so thoroughly that the entire fish including its bones
and head become edible.

Samaki .... Fish

The Swahili-speaking world is a mix of Christians and Muslims. Ham is sometimes served in the
back of restaurants, out of the sight of most customers. "Mbuzi katoliki" [slang] literally means
(goat catholic).

Kiweo/Mbuzi Katoliki.. Ham/Goat Catholic

Kinywaji .... A Drink

Bia... Beer

The adventurous can try Konyagi, a modestly-priced liquor sold in
bottles big and small as well as in plastic packets.

Pombe ....Alcohol

Maji .... Water

Swahili-speaking countries are former British colonies, tea reigns supreme to this day.

Chai..Tea (also slang for a "bribe")

Kahawa .... Coffee

Kahawa Nyeusi ....Coffee Black

Maziwa ....Milk

Mayai... Egg

Chipsi... French Fries

Maharage .... Beans

Mchele.. Rice

Biskuti ....Cookies/Biscuits

Mkate .... Bread

Karanga.. Peanut

Korosho .... Cashew

Tunda/Matunda .... Fruit/s

Nanasi ....Pineapple

Machungwa.. Orange

Embe ....Mango

Mboga ....Vegetable

Nyanya...Tomato

Viazi ....Potatoes

Karoti ....Carrot

Chakula cha Kitanzania .... Tanzanian Food

Ugali...Thick porridge heavy in carbohydrates

Chipsi Mayai ....Mixture of french fries cooked into eggs

Used to pick one's teeth after meals as preventive dental care.

Stiki/kijiti cha meno... Toothpick

The sauce is mild but careful with the raw peppers as the seeds are spicy.

Pilipili .... Spicy pepper

Often filled with sugar and eaten for breakfast.

Chapati .... Fried tortillas/crepes

Often a side of cabbage and carrots (without lettuce).

Saladi .... Salad

Ngori... Banana soup with chewy cow throat

Traveling – from Airplanes to Motorcycles

Bargaining is a necessity; in general, a taxi driver's first offer will be significantly inflated. Taxi kidnappings occur by occasion as drivers force patrons to withdraw money from ATMs until the rider's withdrawal limit is reached. Online ride hailing applications, like Uber, offer non-negotiable fixed prices and drivers vetted for criminal history.

Teksi .... Taxi

Pikipiki .... Motorcycle

Bajaji .... Three Wheel Motorcycle Taxis

Gari .... Car

Kutembea .... To Walk

Ninatembea tu .... I am just walking

Minibuses are outlawed in some cities in favor of cleaner, safer and larger buses, but can be found in other cities. Personal space is at a premium, but the fare price is affordable. Shout "susha" to get dropped off in between stops.

Dala dala (Tanzania)/Matatu (Kenya) .... Minibus

Basi .... Bus

Kituo cha mabasi .... Bus Station

Shuka hapa .... Disembark Here

Ndege .... Airplane

Uwanja wa ndege .... Airport

Mizigo .... Luggage

Huu nimtaa gani? .... This is street which?

Ninataka kwenda + ? .... How do I go + place?

Kushoto .... Left

Kulia .... Right

Formulating a Verb in Past/Present/Future

Subject Prefix	+	Verb Tense	+	Verb Root
Ni	+	na	+	sema

Tenses

Li	Past	Prefix + lisema
Na	Present	Prefix + nasema
Ta	Future	Prefix + tasema

Kuwa – To Be

In Swahili, like in many languages, the verb "to be" is irregular. "Ni" functions as both "am," "are" and "is" while "si" functions as "am not," "are not" and "is not."

Subject English	Subject Swahili	Present Positive	Present Negative
I	Mimi	Ni	Si
You	Wewe	Ni	Si
He/She	Yeye	Ni	Si
We	Sisi	Ni	Si
You all	Ninyi	Ni	Si
They	Wao	Ni	Si

In the past and future – kuwa returns to the normal rules of conjugation.

Subject	Past	Future
Mimi	Nilikuwa	Nitakuwa
Wewe	Ulikuwa	Utakuwa
Yeye	Alikuwa	Atakuwa
Sisi	Tulikuwa	Tutakuwa
Ninyi	Mlikuwa	Mtakuwa
Wao	Walikuwa	Watakuwa

Shopping, Traveling and Past/Future Tenses

Instructions: Cut out individual flashcards. The corresponding words align on the opposing page.

Bei Gani?	Shillingi
Hii, ndogo	Tafadhali
ni	Sitaki
Asante lakini hapana	Kidogo
Ghali	Bei yako ni ghali sana
Punguza bei tafadhali	Asante

Shopping, Traveling and Past/Future Tenses

Instructions: *Cut out individual flashcards. The corresponding words align on the opposing page.*

Shilling	Price which?
Please	This (too) small
Don't want	Is/am/are
A bit	Thanks but no
Your price too high	Expensive
Thank you	Reduce price please

Instructions: Cut out individual flashcards. The corresponding words align on the opposing page.

Ugali	Maji
Chai	Kahawa
Bia	Kuku
Samaki	Daktari
Mwizi	Dala Dala/Matatu
Teksi	Mwalimu
Uwanja wa ndege	Gari
Kushoto	Kulia
Kutembea	Ninatembea tu

Shopping, Traveling and Past/Future Tenses

Instructions: Cut out individual flashcards. The corresponding words align on the opposing page.

Water	Thick porridge
Coffee	Tea (slang for "bribe")
Chicken	Beer
Doctor	Fish
Minibus	Thief
Teacher	Taxi
Car	Airport
Right	Left
I'm just walking	To Walk

Shopping, Traveling and Past/Future Tenses

Instructions: Cut out individual flashcards. The corresponding words align on the opposing page.

Mimi	Sisi
Wewe	Yeye
Ninyi	Wao

Shopping, Traveling and Past/Future Tenses

Instructions: Cut out individual flashcards. The corresponding words align on the opposing page.

We	I/Me
He/She	You
They	You all

Call & Reply – Chapter 4 – Part 4 – A (Questions)

Shopping, Traveling and Past/Future Tenses

Instructions: Reply to the questions below with the appropriate Swahili phrase.

Price how many? ....

I am. ....

It is expensive. ....

We will be.. ....

He was (a) teacher. ....

You will be (a) doctor. ....

That is a car.. ....

Call & Reply – Chapter 4 – Part 4 – B (Responses)

Shopping, Traveling and Past/Future Tenses

Instructions: Reply to the questions below with the appropriate Swahili phrase.

Price how many? ....Bei gani?

I am. .... Mimi ni.

This is expensive. .... Hii ni ghali.

We will be. .... Sisi tutakuwa.

He was (a) teacher. .... Yeye alikuwa mwalimu.

You will be (a) doctor. ....Wewe utakawa daktari.

This is a car. .... Hii ni gari.

Day 5: Questions, Answers and Negation

Question Words

Wapi? .... Where?

Gani? .... Which?

Vipi?... How?

Nani? .... Who?

Kwanini? .... Why?

Ngapi? .... How many?

Lini? .... When?

Nini? .... What?

Yes/No

Ndiyo ....Yes

Hapana .... No

Labda ....Probably/Possibly/Maybe

Je

1. "Je" is used at the beginning or at the end of a sentence to indicate that a question is being asked. Without "je" in the example below, the sentence could be interpreted as a command or as a statement.

Ex: Je, tunaenda hotelini? – Are we going to the/a hotel?

2. "Je" emphasizes the subject of the sentence when placed next to the subject.

Ex: Je, wewe unataka nini? – You (!) what do you want?

3. "Je" as a suffix of a verb means how?

Ex: Ulilalaje? – How did you?

Negative Verbs in Past, Present, Future Tenses

Verbs in present-negative tense do not use a tense marker but the final vowel is usually changed to an "i."

Ku	Past	Hukusema
-*	Present	Husemi
Ta	Future	Hutasema

Negative Prefixes Vary by Subject

Subject English	Subject Swahili	Prefix	Example
I/Me	Mimi	Si	Sisemi
You	Wewe	Hu	Husemi
He/She	Yeye	Ha	Hasemi
We	Sisi	Hatu	Hatusemi
You all	Ninyi	Ham	Hamsemi
They	Wao	Hawa	Hawasemi

Negation

First learn negation for I/Me as it is the most useful in daily interactions.

Sijui .... I don't know

Sipendi .... I don't like

Sitaki .... I don't want

Sifahamu .... I don't understand

Siwezi .... I can't

Usiguse .... Don't touch me (command)

Common Questions – Chapter 5 – Part 1 – A

Questions, Answers and Negation

Instructions: *Fill in the blank with the underlined word in Swahili - Questions.*

Unatoka _____ ? ....You are from *where*?

Mnakwenda _____ ? .... You all are going *where*?

Unaweza kulipa _____ ? ....You can pay how *many*?

Utalala _____ ? .... You are sleeping *where*?

Unataka kula _____ ? .... You want to eat *what*?

Common Questions – Chapter 5 – Part 1 – B

Questions, Answers and Negation

Instructions: *Fill in the blank with the underlined word in Swahili – Answers.*

Unatoka *wapi*? ....You are from *where*?

Mnakwenda *wapi*? .... You all are going *where*?

Unaweza kulipa *ngapi*? ....You can pay how *many*?

Utalala *wapi*? .... You are sleeping *where*?

Unataka kula *nini*? ....You want to eat *what*?

Questions, Answers and Negation

Instructions: *Cut out individual flashcards. The corresponding words align on the opposing page.*

Nini?	Sijui
Lini?	Sitaki
Nani?	Sifahama
Ndiyo	Je, wewe hufahama?
Hapana	Siwezi
Wapi?	Usiguse!
Vipi?	Kwanini?
Labda	Gani?
Ngapi?	Hutaki?

Questions, Answers and Negation

Instructions: Cut out individual flashcards. The corresponding words align on the opposing page.

I do not know.	What?
I do not want.	When?
I do not understand.	Who?
You (!), you don't understand?	Yes
I cannot.	No
Do not touch!	Where?
Why?	How?
Which?	Maybe
You do not want?	How many?

Translations – Chapter 5 – Part 3 – A

Questions, Answers and Negation

Instructions: *Fill in the blank with the word in Swahili – Questions.*

Yes. ....

No. ....

Sifahamu. ....

Sijui. ....

Vipi? .... ?

Nani? .... ?

Lini? .... ?

Translations – Chapter 5 – Part 3 – B

Questions, Answers and Negation

Instructions: *Fill in the blank with the word in Swahili – Answers.*

Yes. ....Ndiyo.

No. ....Hapana.

Sifahamu. .... I don't understand.

Sijui. .... I don't know.

Vipi? .... How?

Nani? ....Who?

Lini? ....When?

Day 6: Time, Date & the Lion King

Time

Time is told differently in Swahili. Day and night divide the day equally in twelve-hour groups. The beginning of the day, sunrise, is "saa moja" (hour one) (7AM), the pattern continues with "saa mbili" (hour two) (8AM). This pattern ends with "saa kumi na mbili" (hour twelve) (6PM) and then restarts with "usiku" (night) at 7PM, also called "saa moja." Perhaps the easiest way to remember is to subtract six hours from the way you are likely accustomed to telling time. Another strategy is to think about the opposite number on a clock. The 9 is opposite the 3 so "saa tatu" (hour three) (9AM).

The twelve-hour segment divides a day from 7AM to 7PM,
as opposed to dividing a day between 12AM to 12PM.

Mchana.. 7AM-6:59PM/Daytime

Usiku 7PM-6:59AM/Nighttime

Asubuhi 7AM-11:59AM/Morning

Saa ....Hour

Saa ngapi? .... Hour how many? (What is the time?)

Saa + x + mchana/usiku .... Hour + x + day/night

Saa + x + na + y + mchana/usiku ....Hour + x + and + minutes + y + day/night

Swahili Hour (Saa)	English Hour	Swahili Declaration of Time
1	7 AM	Saa moja ya asubuhi
2	8 AM	Saa mbili ya asubuhi
3	9 AM	Saa tatu ya asubuhi
4	10 AM	Saa nne ya asubuhi
5	11 AM	Saa tano ya asubuhi
6	12 Noon	Saa sita ya mchana
7	1 PM	Sss saba ya mchana

8	2 PM	Saa nane ya mchana
9	3 PM	Saa tisa ya mchana
10	4 PM	Saa kumi ya mchana
11	5 PM	Saa kumi na moja ya mchana
12	6 PM	Saa kumi na mbili ya mchana
1	7 PM	Saa moja ya usiku
2	8 PM	Saa mbili ya usiku
3	9 PM	Saa tatu ya usiku
4	10 PM	Saa nne ya usiku
5	11 PM	Saa tatu ya usiku
6	12 Midnight	Saa sita ya usiku
7	1 AM	Saa saba ya usiku
8	2 AM	Saa nane ya usiku
9	3 AM	Saa tisa ya usiku
10	4 AM	Saa kumi ya usiku
11	5 AM	Saa kumi na moja ya usiku
12	6 AM	Saa kumi na mbili ya usiku

Leo .... Today

Kesho .... Tomorrow

Siku .... Day

Wiki .... Week

Mwezi .... Month

Mwaka .... Year

Days of the Week

The week begins on Saturday. Note that some days like "Jumatatu" (Monday) are literally
(day three) in Swahili.

Siku za Juma .... Week of Days

Jumamosi .... Saturday

Jumapili .... Sunday

Jumatatu .... Monday

Jumanne .... Tuesday

Jumatano .... Wednesday

Alhamisi .... Thursday

Ijumaa .... Friday

Months

Months are not capitalized in Swahili.

januari .... January

februari .... February

machi .... March

aprili .... April

mei .... May juni .... June

julai ....July

agosti ....August

septemba .... September

octoba ....October

novemba .... November

desemba .... December

"Baadaye" (later) does not always mean (eventually). It is often used
as a polite way to say (maybe) or (no) in response to a solicitation of goods.

Baadaye ....Later

Sasa .... Now

The Lion King

The Disney film The Lion King is rife with Swahili words and can be used as an
easy way to learn some vocabulary.

Simba .... Lion

Rafiki ....Friend

Hakuna Matata ....There are no problems/worries (Don't worry about it)

Nala .... Gift (noun)

Animals - Wanyama

Ndege ....Bird/Plane

Tembo..Elephant

Swala .... Gazelle

Twiga .... Giraffe

Insect .... Mdudu

Time, Date & the Lion King

Instructions: *Cut out individual flashcards. The corresponding words align on the opposing page.*

Later/Maybe/No	Now
December	Bird/Plane
Today	Tomorrow
Lion	Friend
Week	June
Day	Friday
Tuesday	Wednesday
Month	Year

Instructions: Cut out individual flashcards. The corresponding words align on the opposing page.

Sasa	Baadaye
Ndege	Decemba
Kesho	Leo
Rafiki	Simba
Juni	Wiki
Ijumaa	Siku
Jumanne	Jumatano
Mwaka	Mwezi

Chapter 6 – Translations – Part 2 – A

Time, Date & the Lion King

Instructions: Translate the text below, subtract six to determine the time in English - Questions

What time is it? .... ?

Saa moja ya asubuhi. ....

Saa sita ya mchana. ....

Saa kumi na moja ya mchana. ....

Saa sita ya usiku. ....

Saa kumi na mbili ya usiku. ....

Chapter 6 – Translations – Part 2 – B

Time, Date & the Lion King

Instructions: Translate the text below, subtract six to determine the time in English - Answers

What time is it? .... Saa ngapi?

Saa moja ya asubuhi. .... 7AM.

Saa sita ya mchana. .... 12PM Noon.

Saa kumi na moja ya mchana. .... 5PM.

Saa sita ya usiku. .... 12AM Midnight.

Saa kumi na mbili ya usiku. .... 6AM.

Day 7: Common Phrases and Intermediate Swahili

Common Phrases

Concentrate on conjugating verbs for "mimi" (I/me) and "wewe" (you) as many basic conversations revolve around these words.

Q: Jina lako nani?..Name your what? (What's your name?)

A: Jina langu ni..Name mine is.

Q: Unatoka wapi? .... You are from where?

A: Ninatoka amerika .... I am from America.

Q: Unakaa wapi? ....You live where?

A: Ninakaa + mahali.. I live + place.

Q:Unatoka nchi gani? .... You come from country which?

A: Ni/Tunatoka Marekanii... I/we come from America.

Q: Unatoka mji gani? .... You come from city/state which?

A: Ni/Tunatoka Milwaukee, Wisconsin. ....I/We come from Milwaukee, Wisconsin.

Q: Ulifika lini?/wakati gani?.. When did you arrive?

A: Nilifika wiki hii/wiki jana ....I arrived this week/last week.

Q: Unasema/unaongea kiswahili? ....You speak Swahili?

A: Kidogo, ninajifunza kiswahili ....A bit, I am studying Swahili.

Q: Nipe/naomba pesa. .... Give me money.

A: Hamna. .... There is none.

Q: Unafanya kazi? .... You do job?

A: Mimi ni + (kazi gani) .... I am + (job type).

Ex. Mwanafunzi .... Student

    Teachers are privy to a high social status and volunteers are often lumped into this job group.

Ex. Mwalimu .... Teacher

    If people express surprise at your lack of children, do not take offense, it is merely a cultural difference. Claiming imaginary children can help dissuade male attention.

Q: Una watoto? .... You have children?

A: Ndiyo, nina tatu. .... Yes, I have three.

A: Hapana, sina watoto. .... No, I do not have children.

Emergency

Polisi .... Police

    "Mwizi" (thief) is a serious accusation. A person shouting "mwizi" and pointing can prompt vigilantism and a violence against the alleged thief.

Mwizi .... Thief

Nimepotea .... I am lost

Moto .... Fire

Askari .... Policeman/Guard

Toka/Ondoka .... Go out/Exit (Go away)

Daktari .... Doctor

Hospitalini .... Hospital

Terms of Endearment

Bwana..Sir/Man

Mzee..Wise One

Adding the word "yangu" (my) to any noun shows respect and affection.

Mama yangu...Mother My

Askari wangu ....Guard My

Hotels

Hotelini .... Hotel

Mbu .... Mosquito

Chandalua cha mbu ....Net of mosquito

Sabuni...Soap

Karatasi ya choo..Paper of toilet

Ufungua .... Key

Technology

Many technological words like (computer) have two words in Swahili: "tarakinishi" - the proper Swahili word and "komputa" – derived from English.

Tarakinishi/Komputa ....Computer

Simu..Phone

SMS.. Text

Hisa...Internet

People

Mwanamke .... Woman

Wanawake .... Women

Mtu .... Man

Wanaume .... Men

Mtoto ....Child

Watoto.. Children

Family Members

The concept of family in East Africa is more inclusive than it is in much of the world. Even distant cousins are called "kaka" (brother) and treated like immediate family in many ways.

Babu .... Grandfather

Bibi... Grandmother

Baba... Father

When a woman gives birth, she obtains the name "mama" + name of eldest child. She can also be called "mama" + name of other child or "mama" + last name but this is less common.

Mama ....Mother

Kaka .... Brother

These words are often used as nicknames even to those one does not know. For example, instead of saying "mwanamke" (woman), it is common to say "auntie" or "dada" for a woman of similar age even if meeting for the first time.

Dada ....Sister

Baba mdogo .... Father Little (Uncle)

Shangazi/Auntie .... Aunt

Common Words

"Lakini" (but) and "kama" (like) are commonly used words in both Swahili and English. Use them to transition from a beginner to an intermediate speaker.

Kama..Like

Lakini .... But

Kwasababu ....Because

And .... Na

Haya... OK

Sawa .... Equal/Same (Correct)

Sawa sawa .... Equal-Equal/Same-Same

Hii .... This

Common Phrases and Intermediate Swahili

Instructions: Cut out individual flashcards. The corresponding words align on the opposing page.

Simu	Sawa
Lakini	Kama
Kwasa Babu	Na
Hii	Dada
Mama	Kaka
Baba	Bwana

Common Phrases and Intermediate Swahili

Instructions: Cut out individual flashcards. The corresponding words align on the opposing page.

Correct	Simu
Like	But
And	Because
Sister	This
Brother	Mother
Sir/Guy	Father

Common Phrases and Intermediate Swahili

Instructions: Cut out individual flashcards. The corresponding words align on the opposing page.

Daktari	Hotelini
Nimepotea	Babu
Unasema	Watoto
Mtoto	Hamna
Bibi	Pesa

Common Phrases and Intermediate Swahili

Instructions: Cut out individual flashcards. The corresponding words align on the opposing page.

Hotel	Doctor
Grandfather	I am lost
Children	You speak
There is none	Child
Money	Grandmother

Chapter 7 – Call and Reply – Part 3 – A

Common Phrases and Intermediate Swahili

Instructions: Fill in the blank – Questions.

Q: Unasema kiswahili? / Unaongea kiswahili? ..... A: ....

Q: Una watoto? .... A: ....

Q: Unatoka wapi? .... A: ....

Q: Jina lako nani? .... A: ....

Q: Unafanya kazi? .... A: ....

Chapter 7 – Call and Reply – Part 3 – B

Common Phrases and Intermediate Swahili

Instructions: *Fill in the blank – Answers.*

Q: Unasema kiswahili? / Unaongea kiswahili? A: .... Kidogo, ninajinfunza kiswahili.

Q: Do you speak Swahili? ....A: ....A bit, I am learning Swahili.

Q: Una watoto? ....A: ....Ndiyo, nina + x.

Q: Do you have children? ....A: .... Yes, I have + x.

A: .... Hapana, sina watoto.

A: .... No, I have no kids

Q: Unatoka wapi? ....A: .... Ninatoka marekani.

Q: You come from where?...............................A: ....I come from America.

Q: Jina lako nani? ....A: .... Jina langu ni ....

Q: What is your name?....................................A: .... My name is ....

Q: Unafanya kazi?..A: .... Mimi ni + ... (kazi gani).

Q: You work which?...A: .... I am + ... (job title).

Swahili-English Dictionary/Phrasebook

Swahili	English
Asubuhi	7AM-11:59AM/Morning
Asante/Aksante	Thanks
Asante Sana	Thank You Very Much
Asante Lakini Hapana	Thank You But No
Amani	Peace
Baadaye	Later
Bajaji	Three Wheel Motorcycle Taxi
Bei	Price
Bei gani	Price Which
Bei yako ni ghali	Price Your Is Expensive
Basi	Bus
Biskuti	Cookies/Biscuits
Bia	Beer
Chakula	Food
Chakula cha Asubuhi	Food of Morning (breakfast)
Chakula cha Jioni	Food of Evening (dinner)
Chakula cha Kitanzania	Tanzanian Food
Chungwa	Orange
Chumvi	Salt
Chai	Tea/Bribe [noun]
Chipsi	French Fries
Chapati	Fried Tortillas/Crepes
Chipsi Mayai	Mixture of French Fries Cooked Into Eggs
Daktari	Doctor
Dala dala	Tanzanian Minibus
Embe	Mango
Familia	Family
Fanya Hivi	Do This/Do It This Way

Gani	Which
Ghali	Expensive
Gari	Car
Habari	News/What's New [greeting]
Habari Aa Leo	News of Today [greeting]
Halo	Hey/Hello
Hamjambo	You All Do Not Have Things [greeting]
Hapa	Here
Harage	Bean
Hatujambo	We All Have No Things [reply to greeting]
Hii	This
Hitaji	Need/Desire
Hodi	Anybody Home/There
Hujambo	You Do Not Have Things [greeting]
Jambo	Thing/Matter/Problem [greeting]
Joto	Heat
Korosho	Cashew
Ilikuwaje	How Was It/What Happened/How Come
Lala	To Sleep/Lie Down/Recline
Leo	Today
Kahawa	Coffee
Kahawa Nyeusi	Coffee Black
Karanga	Peanut
Karibu	Welcome/Near/Close/Nearly/Almost
Karoti	Carrot
Kazi	Work/Employment/Profession
Kiazi	Potato
Kijana	A Youth
Kisu	Knife
Kiweo/Mbuzi Katoliki	Pork
Kidogo	A Bit

Kijiko	Spoon
Kinywaji	Drink/Beverage
Kitimoto/Mbuzi Catoliki	Ham/Pork
Kituo cha Mabasi	Center/Station of Bus
Kubwa	Big
Kuelewa	To Understand
Kufanya	To Do/Make
Kufika	To Arrive
Kuku	Chicken
Kulipa	To Pay
Kuja	To Come
Kula	To Eat
Kulala	To Sleep/Lie Down/Recline
Kulia	Right
Kuona	To See/Feel
Kuongea	To Speak/Talk/Converse
Kupenda	To Like/Love
Kushoto	Left
Kusema	To Speak/Say
Kutaka	To Want
Kutoka	To Come From/Exit/Go Out/Date
Kuwa	To Be
Kuweza	To Be Able/To Be Capable
Kwaheri	Goodbye
Kwenda	To Go
Jioni	Evening
Machungwa	Oranges
Maharage	Beans
Maji	Water
Maji ya Moto	Hot Water
Mboga	Vegetable

Mbuzi Catoliki/Kitimoto	Ham/Pork
Mambo	Things/Affairs/Matters
Mambo Vipi	Things How [greeting]
Marahaba	I Accept You (reply to "Shikamoo")
Mayai	Eggs
Maziwa	Milk
Mbuzi	Goat
Mbuzi Catoliki/Kitimoto	Ham
Mchana	Daytime / Afternoon
Mchele	Rice
Mkate	Bread
Mizigo	Suitcases/Luggage (2+)
Mkate	Bread
Moto	Hot/Fire
Mwalimu	Teacher/Julius Nyerere's Nickname
Mwizi	Thief
Mzigo	Suitcase/Luggage (1)
Na	And
Nanasi	Pineapple
Ndege	Airplane/Bird
Ndogo	Small
Ngori	Banana Soup with Chewy Cow Throat
Ninyi	You All (2+)
Njema	Good/Fine/Nice (reply to "Habari")
Nyama	Meat
Nyanya	Tomato
Nyumba	House
Nyumbani	Home
Nzuri	Good/Fine/Nice/Beautiful/Pretty
Pikipiki	Motorcycle
Pilipili	Spicy Pepper

Poa	Good/Cool
Pole	My Sympathy/Sorry/Condolences
Poleni	My Sympathy to All of You (2+)
Pombe	Alcohol
Punguza Bei	Reduce the Price (command)
Saa	Hour
Saa Ngapi	What Is the Time
Safari	Trip/Journey/Travel/Safari
Safari Njema	Travel Good (Have a Good Trip)
Safi	Clean/Pure/Nice/Great/First Class
Sahani	Plate
Saladi	Salad
Salama	Safely/Securely/Fine/Peace/Good Health
(Niko) Salama	(I am) Peaceful/at Peace [reply to greeting]
Samahani	Excuse Me/Sorry
Samaki	Fish
Sana	Very/Very Much
Sema	To Speak/Say
Shuka	To Descend/Disembark/Masai Blanket
Shwari	Cool [slang]
Sifahamu	I Do Not Understand
Sijambo	No Thing/Problem [reply to greeting]
Sijui	I Do Not Know
Sipendi	I Do Not Like
Sisi	We/Us
Sitaki	I Do Not Want/I Do Not Want To
Siwezi	I Cannot
Stiki/Kijiti cha Meno	Toothpick
Sukari	Sugar
Tafadhali	Please
Teksi	Taxi

Tembea	To Walk
Tunda/Matunda	Fruit/s
Ugali	Thick Porridge Heavy in Carbohydrates
Uma	Fork
Usiku	7PM-6:59AM/Nighttime
Usiguse	Do Not Touch [command]
Uwanja wa ndege	Airport
Viazi	Potatoes
Vijana	Youth
Vipi	How
Wewe	You
Yai	Egg
Yake	Her/Hers/His/Its
Yako	Your/Yours
Yangu	My/Mine
Yao	Their
Yenu	(2+) Your/Yours
Yetu	Our/Ours
Yeye	He/Him
Za	Of

English-Swahili Dictionary/Phrasebook

English	Swahili
English	**Swahili**
7AM-11:59AM/Morning	Asubuhi
7PM-6:59AM/Nighttime	Usiku
I Do Not Like	Sipendi
(2+) Your/Yours	Yenu
(I am) Peaceful/At Peace [reply to greeting]	(Niko) Salama
A bit	Kidogo
Airplane/Bird	Ndege
Airport	Uwanja wa Ndege
Alcohol	Pombe
And	Na
Anybody Home/There	Hodi
To Arrive	Kufika
Banana Soup with Chewy Cow Throat	Ngori
To Be	Kuwa
To Be Able/To Be Capable	Kuweza
Bean	Harage
Beans	Maharage
Beer	Bia
Big	Kubwa
Bread	Mkate
Bus	Basi
Car	Gari
Carrot	Karoti
Cashew	Korosho
Chicken	Kuku
Clean/Pure/Nice/Great/First Class	Safi
Coffee	Kahawa
Coffee Black	Kahawa Nyeusi

English	Swahili
To Come	Kuja
To Come From/Exit/Go Out/Date	Kutoka
Cookies/Biscuits	Biskuti
Cool [slang]	Shwari
Daytime/Afternoon	Mchana
To Descend/Disembark/Masai Blanket	Shuka
To Do/Make	Kufanya
Do Not Touch [command]	Usiguse
Do This/Do It This Way	Fanya Hivi
Doctor	Daktari
Drink/Beverage	Kinywaji
To Eat	Kula
Egg	Yai
Eggs	Mayai
Evening	Jioni
Excuse Me/Sorry	Samahani
Expensive	Ghali
Family	Familia
Fire	Moto
Fish	Samaki
Food	Chakula
Food of Evening (dinner)	Chakula cha Jioni
Food of Morning (breakfast)	Chakula cha Asubuhi
Fork	Uma
French Fries	Chipsi
Fried Tortillas/Crepes	Chapati
Fruit/s	Tunda/Matunda
Goat	Mbuzi
Good/Cool	Poa
Good/Fine/Nice (reply to "Habari")	Njema

English	Swahili
Good/Fine/Nice/Beautiful/Pretty	Nzuri
Goodbye	Kwaheri
Ham/Pork	Kitimoto/Mbuzi Catoliki
He/Him	Yeye
Heat	Joto
Her/Hers/His/Its	Yake
Here	Hapa
Hey/Hello	Halo
Home	Nyumbani
Hot	Moto
Hot Water	Maji ya Moto
Hour	Saa
House	Nyumba
How	Vipi
How Was It/What Happened/How Come	Ilikuwaje
I Accept You (reply to "Shikamoo")	Marahaba
I Cannot	Siwezi
I Do Not Know	Sijui
I Do Not Understand	Sifahamu
I Do Not Want/I Do Not Want To	Sitaki
Knife	Kisu
Later	Baadaye
Left	Kushoto
To Like/Love	Kupenda
Mango	Embe
Matatu	Kenyan Minibus
Meat	Nyama
Milk	Maziwa
Minibus	Dala dala/Matatu
Mixture of French Fries Cooked Into Eggs	Chipsi Mayai

English	Swahili
Motorcycle	Pikipiki
My Sympathy to All of You (2+)	Poleni
My Sympathy/Sorry/Condolences	Pole
My/Mine	Yangu
News of Today [greeting]	Habari za leo
News/What's New [greeting]	Habari
No Thing/Problem [reply to greeting]	Sijambo
Of	Za
Orange	Chungwa
Oranges	Machungwa
To Originate From/To Come From/To Exit	Kutoka
Our/Ours	Yetu
To Pay	Kulipa
Peace	Amani
Peanut	Karanga
Pineapple	Nanasi
Plate	Sahani
Please	Tafadhali
Pork	Kitimoto/Mbuzi Katoliki
Potato	Kiazi
Potatoes	Viazi
Price	Bei
Price Which	Bei Gani
Price Your Is Expensive	Bei Yako Ni Ghali
Reduce the Price [command]	Punguza Bei
Rice	Mchele
Right	Kulia
Safely/Securely/Fine/Peace/Good Health	Salama
Salad	Saladi
Salt	Chumvi

English	Swahili
Small	Ndogo
To See/Feel	Kuona
To Sleep/Lie Down/Recline	Kulala
To Speak/Say	Kusema
To Speak/Talk/Converse	Kuongea
Spicy Pepper	Pilipili
Spoon	Kijiko
Station/Center of Bus	Kituo Cha Mabasi
Sugar	Sukari
Suitcase/Luggage (1)	Mzigo
Suitcases/Luggage (2+)	Mizigo
Tanzanian Food	Chakula Cha Kitanzania
Taxi	Teksi
Tea/Bribe [noun]	Chai
Teacher/Julius Nyerere's Nickname	Mwalimu
Thank You But No	Asante Lakini Hapana
Thank You Very Much	Asante Sana
Thanks	Asante/Aksante
Their	Yao
Thick porridge heavy in carbohydrates	Ugali
Thief	Mwizi
Thing/Matter/Problem [greeting]	Jambo
Things How [greeting]	Mambo Vipi
Things/Affairs/Matters	Mambo
This	Hii
Three Wheel Motorcycle Taxi	Bajaji
Today	Leo
Tomato	Nyanya
Toothpick	Stiki /Kijiti Cha Meno
Travel Good (Have a Good Trip)	Safari Njema

English	Swahili
Trip/Journey/Travel/Safari	Safari
To Understand	Kuelewa
Vegetable	Mboga
Very/Very Much	Sana
To Walk	Tembea
To Want	Kutaka
Water	Maji
We All Have No Things [reply to greeting]	Hatujambo
We/Us	Sisi
What Is the Time	Saa Ngapi
Which	Gani
Work/Employment/Profession	Kazi
You	Wewe
You All (2+)	Ninyi
You All Do Not Have Things [greeting]	Hamjambo
Welcome/Near/Close/Nearly/Almost	Karibu
You Do Not Have Things? [greeting]	Hujambo
Your/Yours	Yako
Youth	Kijana
Youths	Vijana

Made in the USA
Coppell, TX
11 February 2024

28886484R00057